ONE FAMILY AT A TIME
Gordon Johnson's Story

ISBN 978-0-557-11778-9

One Family at a Time: Gordon Johnson's Story was published through Lulu.com
Books currently can be found at www.lulu.com

ACKNOWLEDGEMENTS

Gordon Johnson would like to thank the many individuals who contributed to the telling of Gordon's story. They include: Gail Biro, Father George Clements, Greg Coler, and Dallas Ingemunson.

Deloris Johnson's careful review of the manuscript was invaluable and Gordon's longtime assistant Kelly Morgan's talent for proofreading kept this project on track.

Greg Milliken
Chief of Staff
Neighbor To Family, Inc.
August 2009

ONE FAMILY AT A TIME
Gordon Johnson's Story

DECEMBER 2008

Gordon Johnson wondered aloud: "Where does it come from?" He struggled to find the right words to explain his tireless crusade to "cure the ills of America's child welfare system."

From his childhood in tough working-class neighborhoods, through the nomadic years of climbing his way into positions where he could make a difference, to worldwide recognition for his leadership in major state and national agencies, there was always one thing that mattered most: "making things right for kids."

Along the way, he experienced personal and professional successes beyond his wildest dreams, and suffered through losses that could have left him embittered and disillusioned.

Even now at 75 years of age, his passion is unabated. It's more than just his genuine compassion for children and families, although that's a big part of the equation. It's also about his belief in human dignity and potential, and his stubborn refusal to ever settle for a lesser option.

Gordon quarter-turned away from his desk, leaned back in his chair, and gazed for a moment at the view from his corner office in the corporate headquarters of Neighbor To Family, Inc. – the not-for-profit foster care agency he incorporated in 2000 in Daytona Beach. He nodded and smiled as a glint of recognition flashed in his eyes. "Well, maybe it all goes back to my father. You know, he was a *very* strong-willed man."

NEW JERSEY – THE THIRTIES AND FORTIES

Gordon remembers Isaac "Ike" Johnson as a firm, tough and passionate man. Although his formal education stopped after the third grade, through his determined efforts at self-improvement he became a respected and influential member of his community. Small in stature, Ike had worked as a jockey in Maryland during the 1920s, before African Americans were pushed out of that profession and relegated to menial racetrack chores. Despite losing his career, Gordon says his father always enjoyed being around the racetrack, and so loved horses that he refused to eat Jell-O, as it was rumored to contain gelatin made from horse hooves.

By 1933, the year Gordon was born in a three-room house in a predominately Italian neighborhood of Long Branch, New Jersey, Ike was driving a truck for Monmouth County. Long Branch was one of the largest cities on the Jersey Shore and from the 1860's to the First World War was one considered to one of the most glamorous resorts in the country. The Great Depression, coupled with new and strictly enforced gambling laws, brought Long Branch's glory days to end. By the time Gordon Johnson's name was added to the census rolls, the city was in a decline that continued for decades. For a time in the 1960s and 1970s it became infamous as a haven for the organized crime organization, Costra Nostra. Only in recent years has the city reclaimed some of former status as a thriving resort community.

Gordon's mother, Edith Greene Johnson, had come to the United States from the West Indies in the early 1930s and found work as a nurse's aide. A tall, warm and genial woman, she never lost her lilting island accent.

Gordon was born in what historians consider the worst year of the nation's Great Depression. In 1933, 27% of the American workforce was unemployed. The stock market was down more than 80% from its 1929 high mark. Breadlines were common. The homeless lived in tent cities, derisively termed "Hoovervilles" for former President Herbert Hoover, whose policies are often blamed for causing the Depression. In that year President Franklin D. Roosevelt would initiate his "New Deal" programs and for the first time the federal government took a leadership role in providing direct relief its citizens.

While the Great Depression affected virtually every group of Americans, no group was harder hit than African Americans. By 1932, approximately 50% of black Americans were out of work. In some Northern cities, whites called for blacks to be fired from any jobs as long as there were whites out of work. Racial violence became more common.

For the Johnson family, and many others, life was very difficult. Gordon remembers the time his parents sat him down in their living room and shared past struggles. "My father was destitute and homeless for a time. I remember him telling me about how to make 'hobo stew' – having learned it as he moved from place to place."

Despite the hardships, Ike Johnson had become greatly disturbed by what he perceived as the Democratic Party's strategy of creating systems of permanent dependence for African Americans. He became a fervid grass roots organizer for the Republicans and assumed a leadership role in his local Elks Lodge. Edith, Gordon remembers, loved to accompany her husband as he made the rounds of local civic events.

Gordon recalls the times his uncle and namesake, Gordon Greene (his mother's brother) would visit from New York City. "He was a staunch Democrat and he and my father would get into very heated discussions. My father was against welfare; he felt it was degrading to blacks and took away their initiative. My uncle believed that the Democrats were helping black people to grow and prosper." After one especially heated debate, they came to blows. "My father kicked him out of the house, and my uncle never came back! That's how strong they were in their convictions."

While Ike's dedicated work for the Party sometimes put him odds with his family, friends and neighbors, he was undeterred in his beliefs and later in life it helped earn him patronage jobs as a deputy sheriff and gallery keeper. Ike's independence and self-reliance, and his mistrust of big government as the total solution to family and community problems, would be a strong influence Gordon's ambitions and world view.

Gordon started school in Long Branch and acknowledges that while he wasn't exactly a star pupil, he was popular and occasionally mischievous. He was also one of the few African Americans at the school. "I remember a time when my friends and I got into some horseplay trouble – it couldn't have been too serious. Mrs. Clark, our principal, brought the five of us up in front of the class. I guess I was smiling a little bit and she came over and smacked me, in front of everybody. Now the entire class was cutting up at the time, so she had singled me out. I went home and told my father, and he went up to school and read her the riot act."

While he was still in elementary school the family moved to nearby Eatontown, New Jersey. Gordon recalls a painful incident from those years: "My father had taken in an older male cousin named Armand. One day Armand accosted me, pulled down my pants and tried to molest me." Gordon escaped and ran to tell his parents. When they returned home from work, Ike and Edith immediately threw Armand out of the house, and Gordon believes the incident sparked his fierce desire "to be a protector of children."

Gordon went on to attend Long Branch High School, played center/linebacker on the state-ranked football team, and became interested in popular music. He decided that he wanted to be a drummer after an attempt at learning piano. "Father bought me my first set of drums and I'd practice three hours a day, wanting to perfect my playing." He was inspired by the "big band" drummers of the day, especially Chicagoan Gene Krupa and Pittsburgh's Art Blakey, and sought to emulate their every "flam, roll, and paradiddle."

From the time he entered high school he was encouraged in his athletic, musical and academic pursuits by a local white couple, Dunham and Wenonah Reinig. Dunham was a Methodist minister, Eatontown elementary school teacher and a former college football player; Wenonah, a homemaker, played piano. They both took a liking to young Gordon and nurtured his abilities. "They saw something in me that I didn't see in myself," he says. Gordon and Wenonah formed a musical duet and began performing around the community at local functions. As Gordon's talent and reputation as a drummer grew, he was selected to perform on "Ted Mack's National Original Amateur Hour" television show.

According to the Museum of Broadcast Communications, the Original Amateur Hour "offered a shot at fame and fortune to thousands of hopeful, would-be professional entertainers. Contestants traveled to New York's Radio City from all parts of the country to sing, dance, play music, and participate in various forms of novelty entertainment. Those who passed an initial screening were invited to compete on the program. Winners were determined by viewers who voted via letters and phone calls, and winning contestants returned to compete against a crop of new talent on the next program. The program's general appeal, reliable ratings, simple format, and low production costs has inspired many imitators in television – most recently, "American Idol." Gordon's appearance earned him a second place. He also traveled to Philadelphia to perform on renowned bandleader Paul Whiteman's television show.

Gordon on the drums, ca. 1953

"After that I started my own dance band and played the proms and dances. I had a rich life and I enjoyed it. The Reinigs had exposed me to wider cultural world, tutored me academically, and later on played a role in my decision to attend Thiel College in Pennsylvania. That positive influence impressed upon me the need for young men and women to have role models and mentors." Decades later Gordon was to return the favor when he and his wife began to oversee the affairs of the elderly Mrs. Reinig, moving her into a care facility near their home in Ormond Beach and extending to her the same patience and attention that she had shown to Gordon.

While Gordon was to be an only child, he says "it was common in those days, especially in the Black community, for people to take in their relatives." In Gordon's teen years, his parents took in a cousin and her four children after the cousin became a victim of domestic violence. Overnight, the Johnson household grew from three to eight. "But it was okay," Ike told his son, "*families belong together*." Sixty years later, those three words still resonate with Gordon Johnson. In them, he sees the seeds of what became his Neighbor To Family program.

THIEL COLLEGE AND THE MILITARY

Turning down a football scholarship at Michigan State University, Gordon took Reverend Reinig's advice and enrolled in 1953 at small, predominately white Thiel College in the rural Pennsylvania community of Greenville. He moved in with the Reinigs, who had relocated there a year earlier.

Thiel College was founded by German Lutheran pioneers who came to the western part of the state in the early decades of the 19th century. Surrounded by the rolling western Pennsylvania hills, Thiel seemed "a very quiet place" to Gordon. At that time, the college had an enrollment of about 600, and he was one of just two African-American students. For Gordon, though, that circumstance just seemed like an extension of his high school years. "I had grown up in Italian neighborhoods, so I was used to living in the white community."

Gordon's academic interests began to revolve around the Sociology and Psychology curricula. He says the smallness of the school fostered close relationships with the faculty, something he enjoyed.

Music continued to play a major part in Gordon's life at Thiel, and at one point he was playing in eight different bands at the same time. "Trios, combos, small bands, big bands – you name it. I was a card carrying musician, and having a great time at it. And you know I never ran into any racial issues playing in mostly white bands." The door to acceptance of black musicians in predominately white bands had been opened in the 1930s by bandleader Benny Goodman, a white clarinetist who hired black vibraphonist Lionel Hampton. Goodman had learned to play his instrument as a boy at the Hull House settlement house in Chicago – an agency that was to later play a major role in Gordon's career.

Asked if he ever consider making music his career, Gordon reflects, "I always wanted to play in a big band, but was afraid of being exposed to that life style," he says. 'That life style' would involve year after year of constant travel to one-night gigs; it led many musicians of that era into alcoholism, drug addiction and disease. "The guys I played with drank a little bit, smoked cigarettes, but they weren't into the other stuff."

Gordon also wanted to play football at Thiel, and did so for awhile, but between the music and studies, it proved to be too demanding. He dropped out of football to continue with his music. "Working in the nightclubs and theaters was a real education," he says. "It was really my first exposure to the workings of power, and the way that power is always held by a select few."

In 1955 Gordon's active, comfortable life as a popular college student and in-demand musician was suddenly interrupted when he was drafted into the United States Army. "I wasn't too happy about it," he laughs. "But it turned out okay."

He was sent to Fort Knox, Kentucky for basic training, then assigned as an infantryman and shipped to Fort Lee in Virginia. Later on he moved to Maryland's Fort Meade.

U.S. Army Infantry, 1955-1957

He spent his two years tour of duty working first as a supply clerk, and then as a member of an honor guard detail, often participating in burials at Arlington National Cemetery.

The Army had desegregated a scant four years earlier, on July 26, 1951. Gordon says that he personally never encountered racial prejudice on the Army, and was, in fact, impressed the number of African-American drill sergeants. He did, however, get his first real introduction to conditions in the still-segregated American south.

"In the south, I had to ride in a different train car, eat in the back of the restaurant." He smiles as he remembers one particular incident: "I had gone with several white soldiers to see Nat King Cole perform in Richmond, Virginia. When we got to the door – in our Army uniforms, I was told I would have to sit in a different section. My friends said, 'we're here together. You let in all of us or none of us.' The theater relented, and I got to enjoy the concert from the 'white' section!"

CLIMBING THE LADDER

Following his honorable discharge, Gordon returned to Thiel and received a BA in Sociology and Psychology in 1958. Gordon had seen that many of the boys he had grown up with had made wrong choices and ended up in trouble, and he decided he wanted to use his college degree to work with and influence young people – as well as those whose job it was to care for them. "Throughout my childhood," he would later say, "I was troubled and dismayed over the way children were mistreated by their own parents and the community."

Armed with his degree and fueled by a desire to help kids, Gordon took his first professional job as a Cottage Parent to 30 youngsters at the 900-bed Jamestown State Home for Boys, a juvenile corrections facility in Jamestown, New Jersey.

He quickly found that the juvenile justice system of the 1950s was far from enlightened, being more custodial than rehabilitative in approach. Significant reforms were not to come until next decade. Gordon told writer Robert J. McClory, in the January 1985 Illinois Issues, that "(Jamestown) was a restrictive, locked-door environment. There was no chance for the kids to develop emotionally or mentally. They were marched to lunch, marched to dinner and were always being counted." He would be forever haunted, he says, by "the look on the faces of groups of children who had been beaten by the guards."

Gordon left Jamestown at the dawn of turbulent 1960s, a decade that would forever change America, especially for its African-American citizens, and would provide focus and direction to Gordon's emerging career.

THE SIXTIES

In 1960 four freshmen from North Carolina Agricultural and Technical College in Greensboro walked into the F. W. Woolworth store and quietly sat down at the lunch counter. They were not served, but they stayed until closing time. The next morning they came with twenty-five more students. Two weeks later similar demonstrations had spread to several cities, within a year similar peaceful demonstrations took place in over a hundred cities North and South. The modern civil rights movement was in full swing.

Four years later, The Congress of the United States passed the Civil Rights Act of 1964 which included provisions for the elimination of discrimination in education, employment, and in public accommodations. President Lyndon Johnson signed the bill into law on July 2, 1964.

One year after that, the Voting Rights Act of 1965 became law, prohibiting the literacy tests and poll taxes which had been used for decades to prevent blacks from voting. According to a 1982 Census Bureau report, in 1960 there were 22,000 African Americans registered to vote in Mississippi, but in 1966 the number had risen to 175,000. Alabama went from 66,000 African-American registered voters in 1960 to 250,000 in 1966. South Carolina's African-American registered voters went from 58,000 to 191,000 in the same time period.

The decade of the Sixties would also transform the way this nation cared for its children.

In 1960, in what became known as the "Louisiana Incident," Louisiana expelled 23,000 children from welfare rolls because they had been born outside of marriage. Although similar actions had occurred in other states, the Louisiana Incident prompted the Department of Health, Education and Welfare (DHEW), which administered ADC, to implement the Flemming Rule, named after DHEW Secretary Arthur Flemming. The rule declared that states could not simply ignore the needs of children living in households deemed to be unsuitable. Instead, the ruling required states to either provide appropriate services to make the home suitable, or move the child to a suitable placement while continuing to provide financial support on behalf of the child.

The 1962 Public Welfare Amendments to the Social Security Act further emphasized the importance of delivering child welfare services to children whose homes were deemed unsuitable. The amendments also required state agencies to report to the court system families whose children were identified as candidates for removal. Together, these provisions resulted in a growing number of children entering out-of-home placements in the mid- to late-1960s. And in 1967,

Congress again amended the Social Security Act to make foster care mandatory for all states.

Against that backdrop of social upheaval and activism, Gordon Johnson set out on a personal and professional odyssey.

In his first stop after Jamestown, he spent two years with the Pennsylvania Department of Public Welfare's Youth Forestry Camp #2. Initially he was a counselor for 7 to 20 delinquent youths that had referred by Philadelphia courts. Soon he was promoted to the program director for entire program, including community relations and camp activities.

Gordon quickly recognized that if he were to succeed in the world in social work, he would need to advance his education. He left the Youth Forestry Camp in 1962 and enrolled at Penn State University, where he was to receive his Master's Degree in Rehabilitation Counseling. Gordon recalls that he was the first African American in Pennsylvania to be awarded that degree, and encountered limited opportunities for job placement in that highly respected professions for whites.

Upon leaving graduate school in 1963, he was selected to be the Assistant Director at Austin McCormic Rehabilitation Camp, a program of the New York State

Division for Youth. As Assistant Director, he was responsible for overall camp program, including counseling, conservation work, recreation, discipline and staff training for 65 youngsters. In addition, he provided counseling for 12 of the residents.

Then two years later, Gordon was promoted to the New York State Division for Youths' Sam A. Lewisohn Short Term Adolescent Resident Training Center, where he served as Residence Director. There he directed and implemented a comprehensive juvenile delinquency program providing psychotherapy, daily care, psychiatric and medical services, recreation and work experience programs.

Gordon's first major career break occurred in 1966, when he was selected from a nationwide search to become Director of Corpsmen Development at the Custer Job Corps Center in Battle Creek Michigan. This was a program that had been plagued with severe mismanagement and youth problems such as riots, gang activity, gambling and other criminal activities.

The Job Corps had been initiated as the central program of the Johnson Administration's War on Poverty, part of domestic agenda known as the Great Society. Sargent Shriver, the first Director of the Office of Economic Opportunity, modeled the program on the Depression-era Civilian Conservation Corps (CCC). Established in the 1930s as an emergency relief program, the CCC provided room, board, and employment to thousands of unemployed young people. Though the CCC was discontinued after World War II, Job Corps built on many of its methods and strategies.

While in Battle Creek, Gordon planned, implemented and directed comprehensive training programs for 1,300 disadvantaged youth, 16 to 21 years of age, with residential living, recreation, counseling and staff training. He headed staff committees, initiated policies and procedures, prepared statistical reports, supervised and trained 231 employees, and supervised finances. He created a safer environment for youth and staff and stabilized the program through a structured accountability program.

In 1968 opportunity knocked once more. Gordon was presented with the first major challenge of his career when he was selected after a national search to launch Miami's new "Model Cities" program.

The Model Cities Program was another of President Johnson's Great Society and War on Poverty programs. Authorized on November 3, 1966 by the Demonstration

Cities and Metropolitan Development Act of 1966, Model Cities originated in several concerns of the mid-1960s. Widespread urban violence, disillusionment with the Urban Renewal program, and bureaucratic difficulties in the first years of the War on Poverty led to calls for reform of federal programs. The Model Cities initiative created a new program at the Department of Housing and Urban Development (HUD) intended to improve coordination of existing urban programs and provide additional funds for local plans. The program's initial goals emphasized comprehensive planning, involving not just rebuilding but also rehabilitation, social service delivery, and citizen participation.

Gordon arrived to find Miami a seething cauldron of discontent. "Tensions ran high and conditions were terrible. Housing was deplorable; there were few good jobs, rampant racial discrimination and poor police-community relations." The economic competition with Cuban refugees who settled in the Miami area during the 1960s further fueled anger and resentment.

Miami, 1968

On the night of August 8, 1968 Richard M. Nixon won his party's nomination for President at the Republican National Convention in Miami Beach, Florida. At the same time, riots in the Model City neighborhood erupted, resulting in four deaths and hundreds of arrests. "As a black man who worked with the city administration's white elite, I was called an 'Uncle Tom' and an 'Oreo'. At one point my life was threatened – I was number 3 on the 'hit' list and the police gave me an around-the-clock bodyguard. "

He remembers that it was the mothers of the community who ultimately stopped the riots. "They swept across the riot areas, rounding up their children."

After the violence quelled, "we were able to get down to business and create a real neighborhood. Roads were repaired and widened. The area's drinking water was rid of pollutants and garbage collection routes established. A supermarket chain opened the area's first real grocery store. Land was purchased for a new government services center. New bus routes were established."

More than thirty years later Gordon returned to Miami to set up another new agency. He was able to walk the streets of his old Model City neighborhood and still see many of the positive outcomes he produced during those dramatic days.

Along his career path, Gordon had gotten married and had two children. Moving from community to community took its toll. It was often difficult for a middle-class black family to find decent housing. "At one of my earliest jobs in Syracuse, New York we were forced to live in a crumbling tenement with broken windows and a carpet soaked through with water."

Gordon and his first wife eventually divorced - their marriage a victim of the stresses associated with their nomadic lifestyle and Gordon's commitment to staying in social work, working for a salary far less than what he might be earning in the for-profit sector. An especially painful part of the divorce was Gordon's subsequent separation from his children.

In 1970 he married Deloris, a Miami medical professional and the woman who was to become his partner in his life and work.

In 1972, Gordon left Miami and the Model Cities program for Pennsylvania to become the Director of the Department of Public Welfare's Bureau of Child Welfare, Office of Youth and Children. There he planned and directed $121 million in statewide child welfare and juvenile court payment programs affecting four regions and 67 counties.

While in Pennsylvania he was also appointed by the governor to serve as Trustee and Past Chairman of $1 million, 12,000-state employee health and welfare fund, and was selected as Acting Commissioner of Office of Children and Youth during the Commissioner's absence. And, Gordon developed and implemented the state's first child abuse registry, "Child Line."

While at an American Public Welfare Association meeting in Washington DC, Gordon became acquainted with Gregory L. Coler, a New York Public Welfare administrator. During a break, Coler mentioned to

Gordon, "I have a job that you might be interested in." That job was working as Assistant Commissioner for Coler in New York's State Office of Children and Youth. Coler was to become a good friend and mentor.

"I was very impressed by Gordon," Coler remembers. "We became very good friends and it has been a lifelong partnership."

"Greg Coler was a confident, assertive leader and I learned a lot from him. He saw in me a potential for leadership, and positioned me – sometimes without me even realizing it – at the right place and right time. The Illinois One Church One Child program would become the perfect example of that." While their styles were very different, Gordon says they were able to work very well together. "They called us the 'salt and pepper' team."

When Coler moved to Illinois in 1979 to become Director of the Illinois Department of Children and Family Services, he asked Gordon to come with him and become his Deputy Director. "Governor (Big Jim) Thompson was very concerned with child welfare and specifically child abuse and neglect," Color said.

"I was reluctant," Gordon remembers. "But what finally persuaded me was that in his new position, Coler reported directly to the Governor. That put me higher up in the chain, with a greater influence on statewide policy than I had in New York."

As Deputy Director, Gordon would direct, implement and coordinate activities with delegated responsibility for children's services statewide, including child welfare, protective services, child abuse, licensing, foster care, and institutional adoption and CETA programs. He also did double duty as Chicago Regional Administrator and represented the director in public and intergovernmental relations.

In 1980, the Illinois Department of Children and Family Services faced a crisis. Over 700 black children in Cook County, including 69 infants, waited for adoption while the agency was unable to find black parents. Coler and Gordon, along with YMCA executive John Casey, approached Father George Clements, a black activist Chicago priest. From that meetings came One Church, One Child, a plan to use the pastors of African-American churches as spokesmen to reach the community. Fr. Clements remembers how it all started with an initial meeting with Gordon and Greg.

"Greg started telling me that the top of their agenda was finding homes for black children who were in foster care, because that was the greatest need," Fr. Clements said. "They asked if I could be of assistance. I said I would have a meeting at my church, Holy Angels, which was overwhelmingly black. I announced the meeting from the pulpit, but didn't get much of a response at all. So I said if I couldn't get any parishioners to adopt, then I would adopt myself. When I actually started to adopt, the parishioners were so shocked by it all that they started to adopt as well. Once we started, we had 69 adoptions in the first week. There was so much publicity surrounding the program, we started getting calls from other churches – it was amazing how it just spread like wildfire." Clements went on to adopt three more boys from foster care, all 11-12 years old.

On the road with One Church, One Child

Coler and Gordon faced several hurdles as they asked a private religious institution to help solve a public agency's problem. They had to change negative attitudes both in the black community; which had grown to distrust the state agency, and among a staff suspicious of change that would implement the black adoption program. They had to revamp state laws that inhibited the adoption process. And they had to change bureaucratic procedures that had proven ineffective. In addition to the administrative side, Gordon and Greg personally met with hundreds of religious leaders to sell the program.

"They really got very much involved in going around to the churches in other cities throughout Illinois, meeting with many groups of ministers," Fr. Clements said.

In late 1982 the US Department of Health and Human service gave DCFS a $150,000 grant to expand the One Church One Child program throughout Illinois. As it grew, the program retained its high public profile, and placement rates for black children began to rise statewide. In the first three years of the program, the number of children waiting to be adopted was reduced by one-half, to 212. A year later it had been reduced to

113. By December of 1986 only 39 black children were awaiting adoption.

Gordon and Greg Coler were involved in many other programs that continue to benefit thousands of children everyday. They worked to change the adoption laws that made it very difficult for black families to adopt. "There was a lot of discrimination against allowing African Americans to adopt in the 60s and 70s," Greg said. "You were not allowed to adopt unless your house was a certain size and if you were married. Foster parents were not allowed to adopt either, another rule that didn't make any sense."

They also pushed for the first modern abuse and neglect program in Illinois. "Sen. Richard Daley pioneered the legislation in Illinois, that included the hotline," Coler remembers. "You could call one hotline number 24/7 to report abuse and someone would be sent out to investigate it. Most states did not have a hotline at the time."

Coler said that changes to Medicaid regulations in the late 1970s under President Jimmy Carter opened up adoptions for children in foster care with disabilities and medical problems. The law was changed to allow children to stay on Medicaid if they were adopted, regardless of their adoptive parent's income. "That really helped adoptions because there were a lot of people willing to adopt, but they could not afford to pay for undisclosed medical problems," Coler said. "Many of the hard-to-adopt children were handicapped and disabled, or had serious medical problems."

"Gordon is not only an innovator in designing programs, but also is an excellent administrator and an excellent leader." Coler said. "A lot of people are creative in coming up with good ideas for programs, but not many people can also administer and lead. Many good programs fall apart because they could not keep the books straight or run it properly. That didn't happen with Gordon's programs."

"Gordon always keeps a positive and upbeat attitude. He tries not to get discouraged, and it is hard not to get discouraged when you work in child welfare."

IN THE 'HOT SEAT'

In December 1983 Gordon was tapped by Governor James Thompson to become Director of the Illinois Department of Children and Family Services, replacing Coler, who had assumed directorship of the Illinois Department of Public Welfare. "This all came out of the blue," says Gordon. "I had no idea that Coler was leaving, and certainly didn't know I had been recommended for his job. I hadn't fully appreciated it, but I had some friends in high places that had confidence in me."

Gordon, Coler and the Governor rode an elevator to the area where the press conference announcing Gordon's appointment would take place. "As I exited the elevator, I momentarily stumbled over the threshold. Governor Thompson turned and said, 'This is not the time to stumble, Gordon. You are on your way to making history.'" Gordon was about to become DCFS's first African-American Director. It merits note that the Governor never once made reference to that "first;" Gordon's long list of professional accomplishments spoke for itself.

With Governor Thompson and Deloris Johnson

Illinois' DCFS was, and is, one of the largest child welfare agencies in the nation. In 1983 the Department was serving some 600,000 children, 100,000 of whom were abused and neglected. "It was the most high-pressure, high visibility job I ever had," Gordon says. "I oversaw a huge bureaucracy with a $500 million budget and 3,000 employees."

Gordon continued to support and promote One Church One Child. In a report for the Ford Foundation, Fred Jordan wrote how he had followed Gordon to a meeting in Peoria, Illinois: "In Peoria, as he has done in Champaign, Decatur, Cairo and elsewhere at the request of the ministers, Gordon Johnson presides at a press conference. He explains the concept of One

Church One Child. Noting that the partnership between the State of Illinois and black churches had made it possible for more than 3,000 children to be adopted... It is apparent that the relationship between Johnson and the board of clergymen is based on mutual regard; their rapport is evident. He respects the ministers for the influence they have in their churches and communities. They respect him for his ability to communicate the One Church One Child message to a wider audience. As is apparent when the 30-second sound bite of his press conference appears that night, the television cameras like him. Schooled in eastern colleges and universities and possessed of a world view formed in part by graduate study and research in the world of social sciences, Johnson appears to be as comfortable in the New Morning Star pulpit as he is the office of Governor James Thompson."

In 1986 One Church One Child was selected to receive a Ford Foundation Award in the Innovations in State and Local Government category. Considered to be among the nation's most prestigious public service prizes, Innovations Awards recognize governmental initiatives that provide creative solutions to pressing social and economic problems. The Innovations program is sponsored by the Ford Foundation and the John F. Kennedy School of Government at Harvard University. "It was quite an event," Gordon recalls. "We received the top cash prize of $100,000. The money and the acclaim took One Church One Child into 22 more states." It was also "the first time the national media took notice of us."

Working directly for the Governor was, says Gordon, an intensive learning experience. James Robert Thompson III is the only Governor in Illinois history to have been elected to serve four terms. "By watching Big Jim, I learned a lot about how things *really* get accomplished in state government." Thompson was, Gordon remembers, "adept at building partnerships with diverse groups, including Democratic Party leadership. I really admired his ability to stay above the fray." Thompson's skills at coalition building served Gordon well the several occasions when he was required to go through a confirmation process. "Some of my strongest supporters were Democrats. That defused any potential conflict."

Overall, though, the decade of the 1980s was a difficult time for DCFS. "I was able to see first-hand what was and wasn't working in the way state agencies handled foster care and other youth programs. Caseworkers were overloaded. Foster parents were quitting at record rates, and the ones who stayed were not always the best possible parents. Both of Chicago's major daily newspapers had chronicled the crisis in a series of front-page articles. And, as the agency's Director, I had to take the heat."

McClory's earlier-referenced Illinois Issues article related "so pleased was Johnson with the opportunity to hold this post that he took a $5,000-a-year cut in salary to accept. Yet Gordon Johnson is sitting on a time bomb, and he knows it. He is the director (of DCFS), a sprawling state agency that is supposed to untangle the knots in other people's lives but has a history of getting tied up in its own. Since 1965, DCFS has had more changes in top management than the New York Yankees. Ten Directors averaged less than two years in office, and if it weren't for Johnson's immediate predecessor Gregory Coler (who lasted five years) the top level mortality rate would be even more alarming."

Later in the same article, McClory noted "(DCFS) is different from child welfare agencies in almost every other state... Elsewhere the state agency merely sets standards for child care, leaving administrative responsibility to the various counties. Hence, the state remains one step removed from the inevitable foul-ups and logjams." McClory then quotes DCFS spokesman Donald H. Schlosser, "(In Illinois) if a case sours, the blame falls right on us. We're very visible."

Among the high profile cases was the tragic story of Natasha Gibbs. Gordon remembers, "She was one-year-old when her mother, a drug addict, allowed a convicted child molester to move into her home. He had already been convicted of involuntary manslaughter in another child abuse case, but nonetheless Victoria Gibbs let him babysit her child. After she left home, the man raped the baby and threw her in the air so violently that her head hit the ceiling. He then beat and violently force-fed her. Natasha's injuries were so severe that she was hospitalized for more than a year and came out a quadriplegic."

The child's aunt had medical training and was willing to take Natasha, but the mother – still drug-addicted and resisted letting the child go. The caseworker was slow to resolve the situation. "I felt guilty and frustrated that our system was failing this innocent child. I had to step in and oversee the case myself, enlisting friends at Habitat for Humanity to build

Natasha a special home and procuring a specially-equipped van to provide her transportation. I also was able to move DCFS, through Medicaid funding, to provide for her special needs. It was but one example of how a tragic case was made even more difficult because of DCFS's monolithic system."

During his years at the helm of DCFS Gordon says he struggled against an entrenched bureaucracy and the unwillingness of both the public and private sector leadership to try new programs for helping youth. Among those he turned to for help was Dennis Hastert, the future United States Speaker of the House.

Prior to being elected to the U.S. House of Representatives in 1986, Hastert had served three terms in the Illinois General Assembly. "Hastert was my 'go to' man in the Illinois Assembly. He was a former teacher and coach who had a real heart for kids, and the ability to advance positions on behalf of the Department." Among their accomplishments, Gordon recalls, were legislative initiatives that improved caseworker training and enhanced opportunities for state employees and foster parents to adopt children.

Dallas Ingemunson, who first met Gordon when he was Deputy Director, became another ally and lifelong friend. "I first met Gordon when I was Chairman of the Juvenile Justice Commission (a position he held until 2006). We became great friends and worked closely on many projects. His DCFS office staffed the JJC, so we had a lot of contact."

Ingemunson, who would become Neighbor To Family's first Chairman of the Board years later, administered federal dollars to help young people in the Illinois Juvenile Justice system stay out of jail, find jobs and lead productive lives. Ingemunson said Gordon served many of the same young people on the child welfare side, so they worked together on many initiatives. Even after Gordon's tenure with state government, he assisted Ingemunson during the massive rewrite of the state's juvenile justice code in the 1990s, "I think we did a lot of good over the years."

"I always admired the tremendous empathy Gordon had for young people in distress," Ingemunson said. "He was a great role model for public officials who served children and families. One of Gordon's great talents is his ability to very quietly urge people to get onboard with his initiatives. He's like a Pied Piper. He has a strong, quiet leadership style that is tremendously effective."

Father John Smith of Marydale Academy had known Gordon for twenty years when in 1995 the Daily Herald asked him by to comment on Gordon's tenure at DCFS. Smith said he "admired Johnson's position, a difficult one in which part of his job was to back decisions to take children away from their families. In this day and age, sending a kid back home can be dangerous; I am glad I don't have to make that judgment. I think he wanted to make a difference for the children, and he certainly did."

"What pained me the most (at DCFS)," Gordon told the Chicago Tribune's Edie Kasten in 1997, "was that I basically was the authority who could take a child out of the home, but I couldn't guarantee those children could be placed in a safe environment."

After seven years in the red-hot glare of the public spotlight, and with Governor Thompson ending his last term in office, Gordon stepped down from his post at DCFS in 1990. He had reached a turning point in life. He was offered, and turned down, a high profile job in the George H. W. Bush administration; he felt that the kind of innovation required to change the system could only happen in the private sector.

"I had come to believe that solving the problems of child welfare wasn't about getting more funding. It was about addressing self-perpetuating bureaucracies, unimaginative management and short-sighted unions – all of which added up to a system that was so rigid and misdirected that it couldn't improve itself."

The opportunity to test this belief came when Chicago's venerable Jane Addams Hull House Association approached Gordon about becoming their President and CEO.

THE HULL HOUSE YEARS

The direct descendent of the famous Chicago settlement house established in 1889 by Jane Addams, the Jane Addams Hull House Association was a Chicago institution and one of the most respected social service agencies in the nation.

The founder, Laura Jane Addams, was born September 6, 1860 in Cedarville, Illinois. She was the daughter of a prosperous miller and local political leader who served for sixteen years as a state senator and fought as an officer in the Civil War.

In 1881 Addams graduated from the Rockford College for Women (where Gordon later became a

Trustee). In the course of the next six years she studied medicine but left it because of poor health, was hospitalized intermittently, traveled and studied in Europe for twenty-one months, and then spent almost two years in reading and writing and in considering her future objectives. At the age of twenty-seven, with her friend Ellen G. Starr, she visited Toynbee Hall, a "settlement house" in London's East End. This visit helped to finalize the idea then current in her mind, that of opening a similar house in an underprivileged area of Chicago.

In 1889 she and Miss Starr leased a large home built by Charles Hull at the corner of Halsted and Polk Streets. The two friends moved in, their purpose, as expressed later, being "to provide a center for a higher civic and social life; to institute and maintain educational and philanthropic enterprises and to investigate and improve the conditions in the industrial districts of Chicago."

Miss Addams and Miss Starr made speeches about the needs of the neighborhood, raised money, convinced young women of well-to-do families to help, took care of children, nursed the sick, and listened to outpourings from troubled people. By its second year of existence, Hull-House was host to two thousand people every week. There were kindergarten classes in the morning, club meetings for older children in the afternoon, and for adults in the evening more clubs or courses in what became virtually a night school. The first facility added to Hull-House was an art gallery, the second a public kitchen; then came a coffee house, a gymnasium, a swimming pool, a cooperative boarding club for girls, a book bindery, an art studio, a music school, a drama group, a circulating library, an employment bureau, a labor museum.

In 1905 she was appointed to Chicago's Board of Education and subsequently made chairman of the School Management Committee; in 1908 she participated in the founding of the Chicago School of Civics and Philanthropy and in the next year became the first woman president of the National Conference of Charities and Corrections. In her own area of Chicago she led investigations on midwifery, narcotics consumption, milk supplies, and sanitary conditions, even going so far as to accept the official post of garbage inspector of the Nineteenth Ward, at an annual salary of a thousand dollars. In 1910 she received the first honorary degree ever awarded to a woman by Yale University.

She became a leader in the pacifist movement and drew heavy criticism for her opposition to the United State's entry into World War I.

After sustaining a heart attack in 1926, Miss Addams never fully regained her health. She was being admitted to a Baltimore hospital on the very day, December 10, 1931, that the she was awarded the Nobel Peace Prize in Oslo, Norway. She died May 21, 1935 three days after an operation revealed unsuspected cancer. The funeral service was held in the courtyard of Hull-House.

According to former Hull House employee Margaret Luft, "The achievements of the Hull House community are too numerous to list, but the impact was incalculable. This group of idealistic young people made Hull House the most famous settlement house in the USA and generated ideas, proposals, and policy reforms still felt 100 years later. Civil rights, women's suffrage, international peace, juvenile protection, labor relations, court reform, public health, public housing, civic watchdog, and urban planning movements can all trace their origins, at least in part, to the work of the Hull House settlement."

But by 1990, Hull House had fallen on hard times. The future looked dismal, and Gordon wasn't sure he wanted the challenge of putting it all together again. Then he took a trip to the University of Illinois-preserved mansion – now a museum – where Jane Addams first established the agency a century earlier.

As he wandered the rooms of 800 South Halstead Street, Gordon felt a genuine bond with the founder. Both had dedicated their lives to "making things right" for children. Both worked in a system where they were relative "outsiders" to the established power structure. And both saw the world as their personal neighborhood. "I realized", he says "that if I took the position, I would finally have the chance to institute experimental programs that might one day change the way the nation's foster care system operates."

"It was time to put my money where my mouth was. I said 'yes' and came to Hull House full of plans," Gordon says. "But first I had to work hard to save the agency. Hull House was barely scraping by. There was a $1.4 million deficit in our $9 million budget, and the board, administrators and employees were at odds."

The esteemed Chicago institution was on the verge of collapse.

Walter S. Carr, a Chicago attorney and Hull House board member, told Dollars and Sense magazine in 1990 that "Johnson grasped the reins very quickly. It didn't take him very long to see where change is needed." Gordon immediately recruited new board members, fired non-productive staff members and hired a public relations agency to remake the agency's troubled image.

The first innovation Gordon brought to Hull House was called the "New Directions" program. "I was always concerned about teens that had been in group homes and bounced from foster parent to foster parent. Often, they lacked the proper life training that prepared them for the 'real world' after they left the foster care system."

In response, Hull House initiated the New Directions program in 1991 with 25 clients. Gordon says, "The program helped these kids in transition to get an apartment, or jobs, or get into college. Counselors were available to them 24 hours a day. They get a stipend from the state, but they still had to find part-time work if they were in school."

Gordon maintained a hands-on approach to New Directions, personally interviewing all of the applicants. In the 1995 edition of Neighbors, the Hull House newsletter, Gordon wrote, "I personally interview each of the 250 teenagers and follow their progress...when they graduate from the program, they return to my office. We celebrate successes and steps – both big and small – to a better productive life."

Betsy Rothstein of the Daily Herald wrote, "it is in these interviews that Johnson gets hit hard with the harsh stories that only inspire him to work harder. 'A sad story is a child who comes in here and says she was raped and had her father's child...or a mother who drops her two children from a seventh-story window. Some come in here with chips on their shoulders just to get accepted,' (Gordon) says. 'I let them know the bottom line: this program is not for you because you have your answers. And that's when it hits home and they come back.'"

By the end of Gordon's tenure at Hull House, New Directions would be serving nearly 300 young men and women per year.

Soon after arriving at Hull House, Gordon was relishing the freedom that working in a private sector setting provided him. In a September 8, 1992 Chicago Tribune letter to the editor, Gordon shared his belief that "Community problems are best solved by neighbors helping neighbors, by people who see the problem up close, who speak the language of the community, and most important, who can solve the problems before they begin. He cited as examples his New Directions efforts and other innovative programs at Hull House, including the "Grandma, Please" hotline which linked latchkey children with elderly volunteers and "Child Care Initiatives," which trained welfare mothers to provide much-needed day care services from their homes and, in the process, transform them from welfare recipients to entrepreneurs.

In September of 1994, syndicated television talk show star Oprah Winfrey announced that she would donate $3 million to create "Families For A Better Life." The program, to be administered by Hull House, would take 100 families from Chicago public housing and provided with an intensive array of services. It brought front-page attention – and 20,000 eager applicants – to the agency. In the fall 1994 edition of Neighbors, Gordon wrote: "With the Families for a Better Life program we're developing a comprehensive curriculum as a framework to empower families to make positive decisions and focus on their strengths."

In addition to the publicity garnered through her hugely popular nationwide weekday show, Oprah's initiative was a featured on the cover October 3, 1994 edition of Jet Magazine and covered by all of the Chicago area media. Hull House's already high profile was propelled into the stratosphere.

With Oprah Winfrey, 1994

From his earliest days in the child welfare field, Gordon had been troubled by the practice of separating siblings that were placed in foster care. "Imagine you are a young child, and you and your brother and sister are taken abruptly from your home by a social worker or police officer. You undoubtedly have your clothes in a plastic bag, and you are sitting in an anonymous intake center. You are filled with sadness and fear, and the only thing that comforts you is that your siblings are nearby."

Gordon continues, "But the forces of the system are working against you, because in another office a social worker is searching for a facility that has extra beds for the night. They might find one bed, or two, but rarely three together. So the family must be split up and the siblings end up being indefinitely separated. That's where the pain comes in." In Illinois, nearly two-thirds of all sibling groups in foster placement were separated from some of their siblings.

So in 1994, as a response to the need for providing foster care that would keep siblings together in their local communities, Gordon conceived of a new program he called "Neighbor to Neighbor."

In addition to keeping siblings together in one foster home, the Neighbor To Neighbor model also addressed a second important issue: the need to create a more professional cadre of foster care providers to work with the increased number of children entering foster care. Changes in society have decreased the potential number of volunteer foster parents. With more dual family incomes needed to meet economic demands, many potential foster care providers are now employed outside the home. The Neighbor To Neighbor model was designed to create professional foster parents who would assume full time responsibilities in return for a salary and a benefits package.

"In many ways, it was the traditional foster parent who ran the old-style system. With their ability to reject placements, foster parents could dictate whether or not siblings stayed together. I wanted to raise the bar and hold foster parents accountable for a level of performance that no one had sought from them. And, frankly, if you can hire someone, then you can also fire that person," he added.

"Recognizing the role foster parents play and giving them 24-7 support is important for another reason, too'" says Gordon. "Traditionally, the turnover rate for foster parents is high – as much as 60 percent the first year. This makes it difficult to find experienced and trained foster parents. By giving them the support they need, they in turn will be better caregivers for our children."

Bernie Mixon wrote about the fledgling Neighbor To Neighbor program in The Chicago Tribune's April 25, 1995 edition. "The Illinois Department of Public Welfare has put $3 million into a South Side pilot program that began last year...the concept is called community foster care. It seeks primarily to keep siblings together in one foster home and in familiar surroundings. Additionally, it promotes mentoring relationships between foster parents and birth parents." The article continued, "There are 72 children – all under the authority of DCFS – being cared for by 20 foster care givers in the Neighbor To Neighbor program....The program places high expectations on birth parents, who are strongly encouraged to work with the foster care providers for hands-on instruction."

Timing for the development of such a program could not have been better. During the 1990s foster care programs across the nation were under attack. Major media outlets flooded the airwaves and filled front pages with horror stories of malnourished, mistreated, misplaced and murdered foster children. The number of children in foster care had doubled in just two decades. Children languished in care without stability or family for extensive periods of time. Primary causes for delays in placing children were the need for parents to complete substance abuse rehabilitation, systemic barriers including overburdened child welfare workers, and resulting delays and postponements of court hearings.

According to authors Dan Schneider and Gary A. Crowin in their book "Leadership in Child Protection" (2001):

(During the 1990s) the media and the public were outraged to learn that children were being abused and neglected in foster care. What's more, foster homes were characterized as unfit environments for children, were frequently over-crowded, and were viewed by the public as merely a financial vehicle for unscrupulous people to use children to make a profit at the taxpayers' expense. There was and continues to be a crisis in foster care and thus a crisis in child protection…. Big government, in which the public had marginal confidence, anyway, was inappropriately intruding into private matters.

On November 19, 1997, President Clinton signed into law (P.L. 105-89) the Adoption and Safe Families Act of 1997, to improve the safety of children, to promote adoption and other permanent homes for children who need them, and to support families. The Washington Post in January 1998 called the Act "the most significant change in federal child-protection policy in almost two decades."

NEIGHBOR TO FAMILY

Bill Ryan was a former Illinois DCFS administrator who had arrived in Daytona Beach in 1994 to manage the local Florida Department of Children and Families office. Aware of the Neighbor To Neighbor program from his days in Illinois, and recognizing the need for programs to improve the local foster care system, Ryan invited Gordon to travel to Daytona Beach and discuss the Neighbor To Neighbor program.

Representative Evelyn Lynn, Chairperson of the State Legislature's Family Law and Children Committee, attended Gordon's presentation. Moved, she quickly became the driving force behind bringing NTF to Florida.

"It is very difficult for children when their parents can no longer care for them," she told the Daytona Times' Kevin Briscoe. "When they are torn away from their siblings the Hull House model becomes a positive reinforcement from which they can benefit when they become adults." Lynn added that the Neighbor To Neighbor model had the potential to replace the Florida Department of Children and Families' current methods.

In the audience at that Florida meeting was one of Ryan's case supervisors, a former Tennessean named Gail Biro. "When Gordon began talking, I thought, 'Of course! This is exactly the way the system should operate!'" Gail was to become the first employee Gordon hired in Florida.

Gordon remembered with irony his earlier attempts to bring a sibling foster care program to Florida. "Florida's child welfare system had been in crisis for several years when Greg Coler was appointed in the late 1980's to head the state's Health and Rehabilitative Services Department. Greg felt that the programs I was starting at Hull House were needed – and would work equally well – in Florida; he encouraged me to try and pilot Neighbor to Neighbor. So during the early and mid-1990s I made numerous trips south, meeting with child welfare officials in West Palm Beach, Miami, Gainesville, and several other communities. They were to little avail until Evelyn Lynn became our champion."

In advance of the implementation of sibling foster care programming, Hull House was given free office space at 1200 Ninth St. in Daytona, a property owned by the Daytona Beach Housing Authority. From this base of operations, Gordon and Gail developed an interim survival strategy by partnering with local agency Stewart-Marchman Center to provide support services to institutionalized youths.

In 1998, the Neighbor To Neighbor program was implemented as a pilot program mandated through the recently passed Florida Statute Chapter, 39.817.

Once again, Gordon's timing was impeccable. From the publication Leadership in Child Protection:

In the late nineties, with the presumed crisis in foster care getting worse and the apparent crisis with in-home services intensifying, the public cost of child protection began escalating sharply. Increasing numbers of children were becoming the responsibility of government and the per-child cost was rising rapidly. A system that already had inadequate operating capacity was being further stretched.

Practice shifted from quickly removing abused and neglected children from their parents and placing them in children's homes, to placing them in foster homes, to emphasizing permanence and adoption. Practice shifted from quickly removing children from their parents, to requiring reasonable efforts with parents to enable their success. The fourth shift, in sharp contrast to those that preceded it, is not linear. Instead, it is multidimensional. Technical solutions are being pursued in many areas and at multiple levels simultaneously. Highlighting a few of the technical changes included in the shift is instructive.

Concurrent planning is a technical change that combines two prior technical solutions. Emphasis on adoption and permanence is combined with intensive in-home services. When a child is abused or neglected by parents, in-home services for the parents are initiated. Since these services may not be successful, planning for the child's permanence, typically in an adoptive home, is concurrently pursued.

Limits on how long children can remain in foster care were shortened. This expedites permanence and deals indirectly with foster care drift and increasing foster care costs.

Training requirements for protective services workers and foster parents dramatically increased. The expanded training focuses on raising technical expertise, increasing knowledge about specific issues, and the complex difficulties of particular children and families. The belief is that more knowledge and technical expertise will help resolve if not eliminate much of the crisis in child protection practice and in foster care.

Managed care became a significant public policy and practice focus. Generally, this technical change moves child protection programs and services from being government-run to being provided by private agencies that contract with the government. This change reflects the publics view that government agencies and personnel are less efficient and less competent than private sector agencies and personnel. The managed care emphasis also intensified the involvement of members of the Children's Safety Net beyond the child protection agency. With that came other emerging technologies such as case management and wrap-around services.

In his usual fashion, Gordon Johnson proved to be both aligned with the most advanced thinking in the field and ahead of the curve in his ability to put into operation programs that addressed the pressing issues of the time.

The initial Neighbor to Family program in Daytona Beach had established four primary goals:

Goal 1: Neighbor to Family will provide safe, nurturing foster care for sibling groups in a home setting and in close proximity to the family of origin.

Goal 2: Neighbor to Family will provide case management and additional services to promote social, emotional, physical and educational development of the children in care.

Goal 3: Neighbor to Family will promote and strengthen attachment between siblings and family members.

Goal 4: Neighbor to Family will provide services of sufficient quality to ensure that participants and stakeholders are satisfied with services.

The Florida Department of Children & Families – District 12 provided the operational funding for the Neighbor to Family site in Daytona, Florida. Gordon recalls that it was not an easy negotiation. "There was definitely a sense that we were interlopers, coming down from Chicago to 'show everybody how to do it.' Finally, it took Evelyn Lynn herself sitting at the table with us and hammering out a fair agreement." Gordon and Deloris use their personal savings to form the non-profit corporation.

The final contract provided for up to $1,879,955.00 over the three-year period. Gordon committed to accept no pay for those three years The funding formula was $55.62 per child per day for allocated services for a maximum of 30 children at any given time. In addition, the Department of Children and Families – District 12 paid directly to the foster caregiver the standard monthly board rate for each child in care. That rate ranged from $369.00 for children 0-3 years of age to $455.00 for children 13 and over.

By that time the program had moved from the public housing complex to a small office in a strip mall on Orange Ave. in central Daytona Beach. "The call came on Christmas Eve, 1998," Gail Biro recalled. "A sibling group of three girls needed immediate placement. Since we couldn't have anticipated the ages of our first group, we were scrambling all over the place getting a crib, clothes, and gifts." Neighbor To Family was off and running.

More placements soon followed, and the program began drawing national attention. A Cable News Network (CNN) reporter came to Daytona Beach and produced a heartfelt three minute report on the program. The Orlando Sentinel and Daytona Beach

News-Journal both gave extensive coverage to the program's start-up, as did at least three Orlando television stations. And in August of 1999 Kathleen Kearny, a Fort Lauderdale judge and newly appointed Director of Florida's renamed Department of Children and Families, visited with a group of Neighbor To Neighbor foster parents in Daytona Beach.

Kearny was so impressed with the program that she immediately wanted to make it a statewide priority. Two districts, one rural, covering Levy, Gilcrest and Dixie counties, and one urban, based in Fort Lauderdale, were selected to be the second and third Neighbor To Family sites.

Unfortunately, after start-ups in both districts, the funders of these new Neighbor To Neighbor programs began seeking modifications to the program model, asking the Hull House group to specialize in non-sibling placement activities such as the recruitment and training of traditional foster parents. Gordon believed so strongly in the purity of the program model that he refused to modify it. Both programs were later phased out, by mutual agreement.

In 2002 the program underwent extensive independent evaluations by both The Ounce of

Prevention Fund of Florida and the University of Central Florida. These evaluations, comprehensive in scope, validated the Neighbor To Family – Daytona Beach program's positive results in child safety, well-being, stability, and permanency. The University of Central Florida report recognized the program as "an excellent example of what programs in foster care can be." The evaluation went on to recommend funding for program replication for siblings and as a model for all foster care programs in Florida. The Ounce of Prevention Fund of Florida program evaluation noted, "The program showed exemplary progress in achieving its objectives and outcomes considering its young age."

Also in 2002, Neighbor To Family was approached about partnering with Casey Family Programs to conduct the nation's very first symposium devoted entirely to sibling foster care issues. About forty selected experts from across the nation attended the 3-day session, held in late May at a Daytona Beach resort. Presenters included Steve Christian, Manager of the Child Welfare Project at the National Conference of State Legislators; R. Susan Dillard, Co-Director of the Children and Family Law Program of Public Counsel Services in Boston; and, the Director of the Casey

Family Programs' National Center for Family Support, Kathy Barbell.

The year 2002 also saw Neighbor To Family establish a program in Fulton County in metropolitan Atlanta, Georgia.

With NTF Board member Linda Klein
and Georgia Governor Sonny Perdue

In early 2004 NTF first deviated from its sibling approach when it was invited to serve children in Orange and Osceola County by the lead agency, Family Services of Metro Orlando. This invitation came after another provider rescinded their proposal only a couple of months prior to roll-out. NTF accepted the challenge of taking approximately 350 children. The focus of the service delivery model was to take the same core values and principles of the celebrated sibling model and integrating them into the expanded continuum of care to include family preservation and adoption services. The narrowed time for preparation was only compounded by three major hurricanes.

In the meantime, the Georgia program had begun to grow and by 2004 encompassed Fulton, Clayton, DeKalb and Gwinnett counties – most of the Atlanta metropolitan area – and was serving more than 200 children each day.

In November 2004, Gordon was selected to receive the Florida Coalition For Children's Distinguished Service Award.

In 2005 NTF successfully responded to a Request For Proposal from Our Kids of Miami/Dade – Monroe – the "lead" child welfare agency for the Miami area. Start up and transiting planning efforts to serve approximately 500 children in the central area were interrupted by on May 26, 2005 when a major service provider pulled out just days before roll-out was scheduled. Just as in Orlando, NTF rose to the challenge and accepted 650 additional children. And once again the roll-out was complicated by three major hurricanes.

As Neighbor To Family grew, the accolades mounted. In October 2006 Gordon received the acclaimed Samuel Gerson Nordlinger Award from the national trade group, the Alliance For Children and Families. This award, the highest given by the organization, was made in recognition of Gordon's "outstanding contributions to the field of child welfare." The same year the agency's Augusta, Georgia office was established, and the following year saw the start of services in Haywood County, North Carolina.

In September, 2007 Gordon was notified that he was selected to be a $100,000 winner of The Purpose Prize, a national award that describes itself as follows:

Unlike any other major national award or fellowship, The Purpose Prize challenges prevailing perceptions by investing significantly in carefully screened social innovators over the age of 60. Each year we award five $100,000 prizes, as well as ten $10,000 prizes, to individuals who have demonstrated uncommon vision, determination and entrepreneurialism in addressing community and national problems. The Purpose Prize will tell the stories of these and dozens of other innovators in the second half of life. Rather than a lifetime achievement award, however, we view the Purpose Prize as a down payment on what these 60-plus innovators will do next.

Purpose Prize honoree, 2007.

Gordon's selection brought Neighbor To Family notice from a host of major media outlets, including USA Today, The Chronicle of Philanthropy, The Hallmark Channel, Miami Herald, Orlando Sentinel and many others.

As Gordon approaches his 76th birthday, he shows no signs of slowing down. A major research paper from the University of Georgia confirmed that the Neighbor To Family model had withstood the test of time and growth. Programs are in works for Ohio and Texas. His travel schedule would wear down people half his age.

He is busy writing the next chapter, one family at a time.